D1442607

MILITARY AIRCRAFT

UAVs
UNMANNED AERIAL
VEHICLES

BY JOHN HAMILTON

VISIT US AT
WWW.ABDOPUBLISHING.COM

Published by ABDO Publishing Company, PO Box 398166, Minneapolis, MN 55439.
Copyright ©2012 by Abdo Consulting Group, Inc. International copyrights reserved in all countries. No part of this book may be reproduced in any form without written permission from the publisher. A&D Xtreme™ is a trademark and logo of ABDO Publishing Company.

Printed in the United States of America, North Mankato, Minnesota.
122011
012012

 PRINTED ON RECYCLED PAPER

Editor: Sue Hamilton
Graphic Design: Sue Hamilton
Cover Design: John Hamilton
Cover Photo: United States Air Force
Interior Photos: AeroVironment, Inc-pg 28 (inset); Corbis-pgs 10-11; Defense Video & Imagery Distribution System-pgs 1, 2-3, 6 (inset), 8, 9, 24-25, 26-27 & 32; Getty Images-pgs 28-29; Northrop Grumman-pgs 22-23; United States Air Force-pgs 4-7, 12-21 & 30-31.

ABDO Booklinks
Web sites about Military Aircraft are featured on our Book Links pages. These links are routinely monitored and updated to provide the most current information available.
Web site: www.abdopublishing.com

Library of Congress Cataloging-in-Publication Data

Hamilton, John, 1959-
UAVs : unmanned aerial vehicles / John Hamilton.
    p. cm. -- (Xtreme military aircraft)
Includes index.
Audience: Ages 8-15.
ISBN 978-1-61783-271-0
1. Drone aircraft--United States--Juvenile literature. I. Title. II. Title: Unmanned aerial vehicles.
UG1242.D7H36 2012
623.74'69--dc23
                    2011042339

TABLE OF CONTENTS

UAVs ★★★

Unmanned Aerial Vehicles (UAVs) are aircraft that have no pilot or are remotely controlled. They can carry cameras, sensors, cargo, or even weapons. These spy planes are now heavily used by the United States armed forces.

Live UAV battlefield footage helps commanders make better-informed decisions about troop movements, timing, and targeting.

An MQ-1B Predator UAV takes off on a spy mission from Balad Air Base in Iraq.

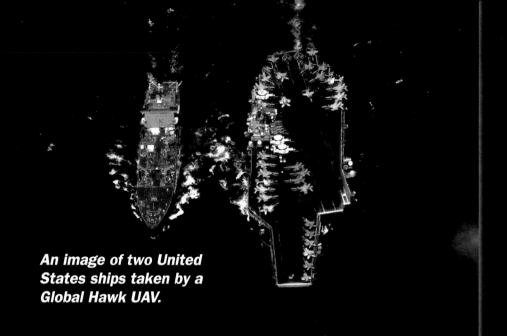

An image of two United States ships taken by a Global Hawk UAV.

An RQ-4 Global Hawk UAV waits to take off on a mission.

The most important job of a UAV is reconnaissance. UAVs give soldiers a real-time bird's-eye view of the battlefield. UAVs can fly high in the air for a long time. They send high-resolution images to ground operators, who may be thousands of miles away in a safe location.

XTREME FACT

If a UAV is shot down or accidentally crashes, there is no pilot to worry about.

UAVs come in many different shapes and sizes. Some are as small as toy airplanes. Soldiers can launch them by hand.

A U.S. Army soldier launches a Raven UAV.

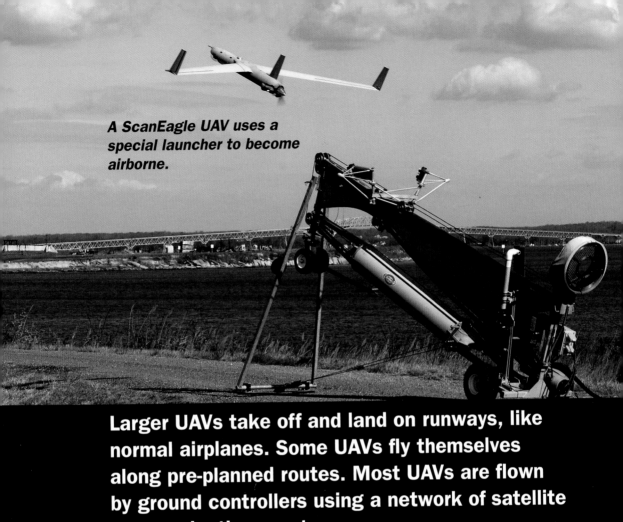

A ScanEagle UAV uses a special launcher to become airborne.

Larger UAVs take off and land on runways, like normal airplanes. Some UAVs fly themselves along pre-planned routes. Most UAVs are flown by ground controllers using a network of satellite communications systems.

Fire Scout UAVs can take off and land from the flight decks of U.S. Navy ships.

HISTORY

The idea for pilotless drones began almost as soon as planes were invented. During World War II, the U.S. built several drones. UAVs were used to spy on the enemy during the Vietnam War. As the U.S. became involved in wars in the Middle East in the 1990s and 2000s, it added several advanced types of UAVs to its fleet of aircraft.

*United States troops
test drones at Chu Lai,
Vietnam, in 1968.*

PREDATOR

The MQ-1B Predator is a U.S. Air Force medium-altitude, long-range UAV. It can stay in the air for up to 24 hours. It looks like a small airplane with long wings. It takes off and lands from a runway.

Using advanced optics, the Predator can shoot video from a very high altitude. It also uses infrared imaging to see at night or through smoke or clouds.

A U.S. Air Force major operates the virtual cockpit of a Predator at a base in Afghanistan.

13

Predators can be armed with Hellfire missiles. It is a precision-guided weapon. The UAV "paints" a ground target with a laser beam, which guides the missile. These deadly drones are used today in remote areas such as Afghanistan or Pakistan.

A Predator flies an armed reconnaissance mission in a remote area.

Predator Specifications

Length:	27 feet (8.2 m)
Height:	6.9 feet (2.1 m)
Wingspan:	55 feet (16.8 m)
Weight:	1,130 pounds (513 kg)
Cruising Speed:	84 miles per hour (135 kph)
Range:	770 miles (1,239 km)
Ceiling:	25,000 feet (7,620 m)

REAPER

The MQ-9 Reaper is larger and more powerful than the Predator. It can fly at a height of 50,000 feet (15,240 m). That is beyond the range of most anti-air missile defenses. The Reaper uses high-resolution imaging systems to spot the enemy.

An MQ-9 Reaper ready to launch in Afghanistan.

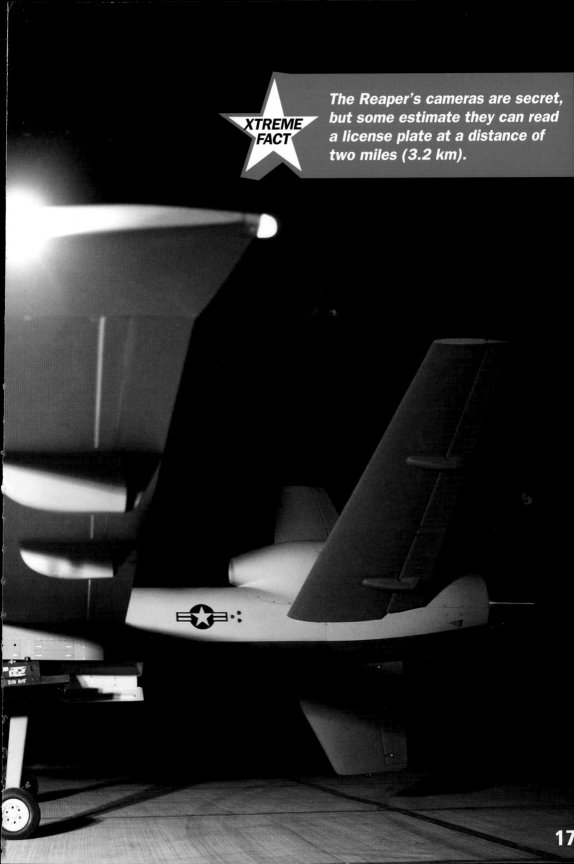

The Reaper's cameras are secret, but some estimate they can read a license plate at a distance of two miles (3.2 km).

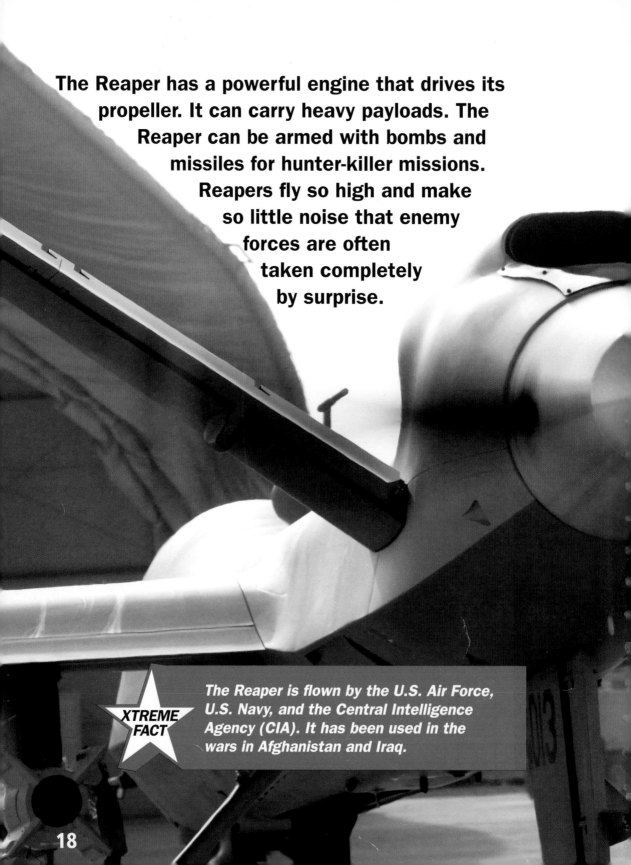

The Reaper has a powerful engine that drives its propeller. It can carry heavy payloads. The Reaper can be armed with bombs and missiles for hunter-killer missions. Reapers fly so high and make so little noise that enemy forces are often taken completely by surprise.

XTREME FACT

The Reaper is flown by the U.S. Air Force, U.S. Navy, and the Central Intelligence Agency (CIA). It has been used in the wars in Afghanistan and Iraq.

Reaper Specifications:

Length:	36 feet (11 m)
Height:	12.5 feet (3.8 m)
Wingspan:	66 feet (20.1 m)
Weight:	4,900 pounds (2,223 kg)
Cruising Speed:	230 miles per hour (370 kph)
Range:	1,150 miles (1,851 km)
Ceiling:	50,000 feet (15,240 m)

Reapers can carry AGM-114 Hellfire missiles, GBU-12 Paveway II laser-guided bombs, and GBU-38 Joint Direct Attack Munitions.

19

GLOBAL HAWK

An RQ-4 Global Hawk flies
a mapping mission over
Central America.

XTREME FACT

The Global Hawk is powered by a
Rolls-Royce AE 3007H turbofan
jet engine mounted on the back of
the UAV.

The United States Air Force RQ-4 Global Hawk is a high-altitude UAV. It can travel long distances. It can fly over the battlefield for as long as 42 hours. Its cameras, sensors, and radar can detect enemy forces during the day or at night, even through clouds or smoke.

An image of Southern California fires taken by an RQ-4 Global Hawk to help firefighters.

U.S. AIR FORCE

The Global Hawk can use satellites to communicate with ground operators a continent away. Operators include a pilot to fly the UAV. A second operator controls the Global Hawk's sensors.

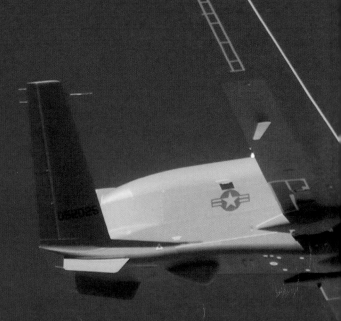

The Global Hawk will eventually replace the manned U2 spy plane. The UAV has often been used in the wars in Iraq and Afghanistan.

Global Hawk Specifications:

Length:	47.6 feet (14.5 m)
Height:	15.3 feet (4.7 m)
Wingspan:	130.9 feet (39.9 m)
Weight:	14,950 pounds (6,781 kg)
Cruising Speed:	357 miles per hour (575 kph)
Range:	10,012 miles (16,113 km)
Ceiling:	60,000 feet (18,288 m)

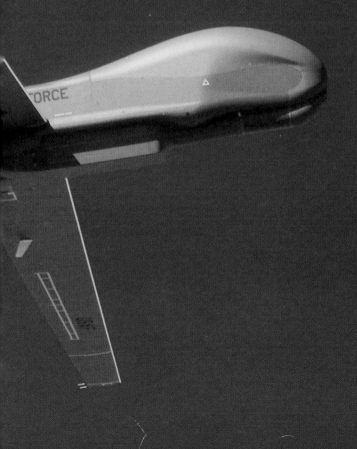

FIRE SCOUT

The MQ-8 Fire Scout UAV doesn't need a runway. It takes off and lands vertically, like a helicopter. It can land on U.S. Navy ships, even in windy weather. The Fire Scout can detect enemy ground troops, ships, or submarines. It can also be armed with Hellfire missiles or rockets. The Fire Scout has been used on surveillance missions in Afghanistan and Libya.

Fire Scout Specifications:

Length:	24 feet (7.3 m)
Height:	9.7 feet (3 m)
Rotor Diameter:	27.5 feet (8.4 m)
Weight:	2,073 pounds (940 kg)
Cruising Speed:	124 miles per hour (200 kph)
Range:	127 miles (204 km)
Endurance:	8 hours
Ceiling:	20,000 feet (6,096 m)

A Fire Scout hovers over the deck of the USS McInerney.

In 2010, a Fire Scout detected drug smugglers in a speedboat in the eastern Pacific Ocean. The U.S. Navy soon captured them.

RAVEN

The RQ-11 Raven is a small UAV. It weighs only 4.2 pounds (1.9 kg). Soldiers launch it by hand.

It is powered by an electric motor. It can fly for several miles and spy on nearby enemy forces. Ravens are used by the United States Army, Marines, and Air Force.

A United States Army sergeant prepares to launch a Raven UAV in Afghanistan.

More than 13,000 Raven airframes have been built. They are used by U.S. troops and the armed forces of allied countries such as Great Britain, Denmark, and Australia.

Raven Specifications:

Length:	36 inches (91 cm)
Wingspan:	55 inches (140 cm)
Weight:	4.2 pounds (1.9 kg)
Cruising Speed:	35 miles per hour (56 kph)
Range:	6.2 miles (10 km)
Ceiling:	10,000 feet (3,048 m)

THE FUTURE

A Hummingbird UAV is being tested for reconnaissance use.

Many countries use UAVs. New models are tested each year. Some are as small as hummingbirds or insects. Some larger UAVs use stealth technology. The U.S. Air Force RQ-170 Sentinel resembles a small version of the B-2 Spirit stealth bomber.

An RQ-170 Sentinel, which looks like a small version of the B-2 Spirit stealth bomber, on display at an air show.

Pilotless UAVs may someday replace expensive fighter aircraft. For now, they remain important "eyes in the sky." They are an indispensable part of modern warfare.

GLOSSARY

AIRFRAME
The body of an aircraft, minus its engine.

CENTRAL INTELLIGENCE AGENCY
The Central Intelligence Agency's (CIA) mission is to collect information, such as reports, photos, or video, from foreign countries. It often collects this information covertly. Covert means to do something while staying hidden. A UAV that takes photos from high in the sky is one example of covert information gathering. The CIA then evaluates this information and puts it in a report, which is given to the president of the United States and other government officials.

INFRARED
Part of the electromagnetic spectrum that has wavelengths that are too long to be part of visible light. Infrared light includes thermal radiation, or heat.

PRECISION-GUIDED WEAPON
Precision-guided weapons, also called "smart bombs," are bombs or missiles that can be steered in mid-air toward their targets. Some UAVs can launch several kinds of precision-guided weapons, or "munitions." These include bombs and missiles that are guided by lasers, radar, or satellite signals.

RADAR

A way to detect objects, such as aircraft or ships, using electromagnetic (radio) waves. Radar waves are sent out by large dishes, or antennas, and then strike an object. The radar dish then detects the reflected wave, which can tell operators how big an object is, how fast it is moving, its altitude, and its direction.

STEALTH TECHNOLOGY

Some advanced aircraft today use stealth technology to make them nearly invisible to enemy radar. They are constructed with smooth, curving surfaces, with few jagged edges to reflect radar waves. They also are constructed of material that absorbs radar. Certain coatings applied to the aircraft also absorb radar. The United States Air Force B-2 Spirit and F-35 multirole fighter are aircraft that use stealth technology.

VIETNAM WAR

A conflict between the countries of North Vietnam and South Vietnam from 1955-1975. Communist North Vietnam was supported by China and the Soviet Union. The United States entered the war on the side of South Vietnam.

WORLD WAR II

A war that was fought from 1939 to 1945, involving countries around the world. The United States entered the war after Japan's bombing of the American naval base at Pearl Harbor, in Oahu, Hawaii, on December 7, 1941.

INDEX

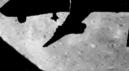